DISCLAIMER

This fine handbook is in no way restricted to individuals capable of fever blister production. Furthermore, it is not mandatory you currently have an outbreak to continue. For those of you fortunate enough to have never been visited by the Fever Blister Fairy, there is no risk you will be infected by reading this book.

The Fever Blister Handbook

The Fever Blister Handbook

Josef J. Hoskins

Page 32 Publishing

The Fever Blister Handbook by Josef J. Hoskins

Published by Page 32 Publishing

Copyright © 2015 by Josef J. Hoskins

Cover Design by: Josef J. Hoskins and Wendell Hess

ISBN: 978-0692535578

josefjhoskins.com

For my siblings and for all whose
lips are a garden bearing that
most wicked vegetation.

"…knowing is half the battle."
– G.I. Joe

Table o' Contents

Prodrome

He awoke with a start as the morning sun crept into the stillness of the bedroom. After an involuntary yawn and satisfying stretch, he glanced about the room and was surprised to find drastic changes. The beige curtains had been replaced by a dark brown variation and the bed now faced a different wall.

His eyes widened as a sudden horror enveloped him. "How long have I slept?" he wondered.

Though still somewhat groggy, he leapt to his feet and rummaged for a calendar atop the nearby dresser. Trinkets and decorations were thrown aside as he worked frantically to quell his fears. "Who knows what I've missed," he said to himself.

As he swept over to the desk and foraged through the drawers, a bedside radio came to life. The DJ fired off a few local news headlines and then transitioned into a brief weather forecast.

Abandoning his search, he whipped around to glare at the radio. "Come on, say the date. Say it!"

The DJ wrapped his commentary declaring, "Looks like our last weekend of July is gonna be a hot one."

"Yes!" he declared as he focused his attention back to the desk. Partially relieved by learning the date, his investigation grew less hectic and finally bore fruit. He discovered a pocket-sized monthly planner he previously overlooked. Surveying the tool that helped him so many times in the past, he could not help but feel optimistic and nervous at the same time.

"Let me see," he thought to himself. "The last thing I can remember is the Christmas party. That in itself is utterly ridiculous. I don't usually sleep so long." He took a moment to shake a fist skyward and bellow, "Why?"

He hastily opened the planner and flipped pages while scanning for any scribbled notes. Just as he feared, a bountiful smattering of prime social events popped up like…well…popcorn.

"Oh, how lovely. A dinner with old college friends, birthday parties, work meetings, a family portrait and the annual 4th of July neighborhood cookout." He recited the missed opportunities aloud as a form of punishment. "This is just great! I've probably missed running into an ex at the grocery store too!"

"Curse my slothfulness!" he shouted and slung the planner against the wall. After pounding the dresser with his fist, he dropped his head in defeat. He inhaled sharply through his nose and closed his eyes, taking a moment to regroup. When he finally relaxed and lifted his head, he spotted a scrap of paper on the floor.

"What's this?" he muttered as he leaned down to examine his find.

Within seconds, all his prior frustration evaporated. "Saturday. Eight o'clock. High school reunion!"

Excitement rose in his voice like a crescendo as he read those precious words. This was just what he needed. This made up for all the missed time. He plopped down on the side of the bed and sighed heavily, content all was not lost.

"Awww yeah," he said to himself as he smiled at the note. With a smug look over at his unwitting host, he added, "*We'll* be there."

1

Just So You Know

You may have realized immediately the prologue you just read was an imagined day in the life of a fever blister. But then again, maybe you didn't. And yes, I know it was called "prodrome" instead of "prologue". That was a little joke. Maybe you thought it was funny. But then again, maybe you didn't. If you don't know what a prodrome is, you might have a laugh about it later when you become more acquainted with the term. But then again…okay I'll stop that now.

Before you embark on your path toward fever blister enlightenment, allow me to prepare you with another piece of preliminary information. I'm going to be all presumptuous and assume if you have decided upon reading this heartwarming handbook, you are at least somewhat familiar with this enemy of the face.

Your experience may be personal or not, but I'm going to pretend you have not opened this book looking for an in-depth medical commentary. You will notice I have, ever so slightly, included a few morsels of relevant medical information. But if you have chosen to peruse this incredibly awesome guide with an unexplainable hunger for knowledge about epidemiology and what not, you may be disappointed. You can look that crap up on your own.

I will, however, serve up a couple of initial statistical tidbits just to illustrate the desperate need the world has for this book. According to a recent report by the World Health Organization, it is estimated two thirds of our fair planet's humankind under the age of 50 are infected with the virus that spawns the vile matter known as fever blisters. Whether asymptomatic or not, that's close to four *billion* people. You should have read the last few words of the preceding sentence with your best Dr. Evil impersonation. If not, go back and do it now.

Anyway, that's about all I will say about such things. The material compiled within these pages is meant to be helpful and entertaining. I mean let's face it, if you are one of us chosen by the face darkness, you should have already accepted the fact you have been marked. No amount of statistical data will do you any good.

In place of endless medical babbling, this fantastic handbook features the insight, observations and advice gathered from those who routinely play host to that scourge of the labial landscape. And if you haven't surmised by now, the aim is to present this information in a fashion most humorous.

Enjoy your journey.

2

They Who Must Be Named

Fever blisters are an infection caused by type 1 of the herpes simplex virus (HSV-1). This infection chooses the highly visible location of your lips and/or greater mouth region as a place to call home. A not-so-random sample of those afflicted propose this happening is due to the exhibitionistic nature of the virus. Whether or not this theory holds water, the curse of wearing random herpes outbreaks on your face allows everyone you encounter to involuntarily share in the experience with you.

The publicity of these disgusting eruptions is one of the main reasons this amazing handbook was created. This is a dilemma that has always been out in the open, though many choose to ignore or overlook it. I realize the subject may be embarrassing for some, but it is one that needs to be addressed.

The blisters themselves, those crazy little guys, are a reactivation of the herpes simplex virus. HSV-1 is one of those gifts that keep on giving because the freeloading virus never leaves your body after the primary infection. Lucky us, huh?

Common causes of the recurrent outbreaks include stress, sunburn, fever, menstruation, dehydration and my personal belief: for absolutely no reason whatsoever. In those precious periods of dormancy, the herpes gathers its strength and plots a return for what it considers the most opportune moments. This will be discussed in greater detail later.

Though fever blisters are also referred to as "cold sores", allow me to offer a review of the medical lingo. In that camp, you'll find names even more unflattering such as herpes simplex labialis, recurrent herpes labialis and orolabial herpes.

I'm guessing you'd prefer to avoid supplying anyone with the knowledge you've got a little case of herpes labialis. Or perhaps you're someone who likes that sort of attention. If you side with the former, I recommend you invent some fun nicknames for your hangers-on. Sound good? Yeah, I thought so.

Be advised this practice has not been proven to affect the herpes on an emotional or physical level, but at least you'll be able to personalize your fever blisters. And perhaps, through clever usage, you can make others more comfortable with those crusty extensions of your lip.

On the next page you will be treated to examples of popular fever blister nicknames, gathered from a minimal amount of research.

The Examples of Nicknames I Just Mentioned:

- Little Friend
- Crusty Buddy
- Vile Visitor
- Wingman
- Bubbly Bling
- Face Décor
- Face Accessory
- Face Crustacean
- Liphugger
- Lip Ornament
- Lip Lover
- Lip Barnacle
- Window to the Dark Place

While this list is admittedly marvelous, it's also just a pinch of the possible monikers. Use these examples to inspire you. I'm sure you can come up with a variety of your own endearing titles for your herpes.

3

Classification

Folks unlearned in herpes lore might be susceptible to the belief there is only one type of fever blister. Those of us in the know find this assumption laughable. Our firsthand experience has taught us the herpes can assume many forms when assaulting the face. Try to spot your most common manifestation in the following categories.

1. Conventional: this brand of herpes only pops up when you attend a convention. I'm only kidding. Conventional herpes are run-of-the-mill blisters. These are the most common type, average in both size and appearance. By the way, "Conventional Herpes" would be an excellent band name. If you're interested, let me know and we can work out my royalties.

2. Rebellious: this type likes to break away from the norm. He does not fancy the idea of following the herd...of herpes. I have to admit I'm curious what images sprang to mind when you read the words "herd of herpes". Anyway, this variety does not want anyone to think he's dependent on the lip for survival. Rebellious blisters are commonly noted a short distance away from the lips, but still in the vicinity. Far enough to say he's left home, but not a significant distance. It's probably just a phase.

3. Nomadic: blisters of this ilk crave adventure and exploration. Similar to the Rebellious faction in regard to thinking outside the lip, the Nomadic herpes differentiate themselves with their passion for journeying greater distances and locating new places to settle. You will notice these wayfaring crusters popping up in unusual locations such as the bottom edge of the nostrils.

4. Colony: while this breed is surprisingly a singular outbreak, it does present itself that way. Colonial blisters have an insatiable lust for real estate. This type typically appears as a massive manifestation, such as a happy little herpes village that occupies one whole corner of your mouth.

5. Clingy: these are the blisters that just can't say "goodbye". The lingering scab hangs by a mere thread, but you know all too well if you choose to sever that thread, you're going to pay for your foolish eagerness with a bloody lip and another scab rising to take its place.

6. Echo: sometimes called a "teaser blister", Echoes are mysterious types that never actually surface beyond a reddened area on or around the lip. Did the herpes change its mind? Was it a ghost of herpes past? Perhaps a whisper of herpes still yet to come? We may never know. Just be happy about it.

These classifications may seem comprehensive, but when you are dealing with the herpes you can never take anything for granted. The viralness may yet evolve and present itself in new and even more hideous iterations. You have been warned.

4

That Tingling Sensation

Anyone who is afflicted can attest to the odd fact fever blisters come with a sort of sixth sense. For those who don't understand what I'm sayin', prepare to receive an elaboration. Sorry about that. Sometimes I bust rhymes. I can't help myself.

Before a fever blister actually rears its bubbly head, victims commonly experience an acute tingling, itching or burning sensation on the lip where the herpes will soon birth its nasty self into the world. In medical terms this symptom is called a "prodrome". Remember when I mentioned this earlier? I do.

If your response time in deploying a method of treatment is swift, the longevity of the blister might be greatly reduced. Other times your efforts are all for naught. It all depends on the strength and/or mood of the herpes. Either way, that peculiar tingling may continue intermittently during the fever blister's lifespan.

All attempts to understand the significance of these "signals" have ended in disappointment. Findings were inconclusive at best. The general consensus of the two or three researchers assigned to the project was the herpes likes to keep you guessing. On the bright side (yes, there can still be a bright side even when the lip nemesis has your number), you can capitalize on this foreshadowing of evil to change upcoming social engagements.

For a bit of fun, I like to pretend the phenomenon is similar to Spider-Man's "spider sense". Sadly, I cannot report the random occurrences of the tingling sensation have ever indicated a warning of danger. The instances are usually just interpreted as a reminder to apply another slathering of medication. However, these transmissions from our lips may very well be the herpes attempting to communicate. While this is unlikely, your blister could be trying to tell you something important. Or it may only want to express approval for what you're watching on television. I don't think we'll ever know for sure.

5

Enter the Herpes

A noted scholar once drew a comparison between fever blisters and their imminent appearances to those Final Destination films. In said films, the characters attempt to cheat Death, but the Reaper always manages to claim his intended victims in the end.

This concept is not unlike the experience of being perpetually haunted by the herpes. Though you might lessen the impact of a manifestation through assorted tactics or be fortunate enough to have a false alarm, the Grim Blister will not be denied. He will return. Oh yes, he will return…and he will be angry.

Anyone who experiences recurrent visits from the herpes realm knows fever blisters have a rather uncanny ability to show up just in time for special events (see the handy frequency chart on page 18). Despite the herpes possessing this despicable sense of timing, it is not above making mistakes. Sometimes your vile visitor becomes a

Fever Blister Frequency Chart

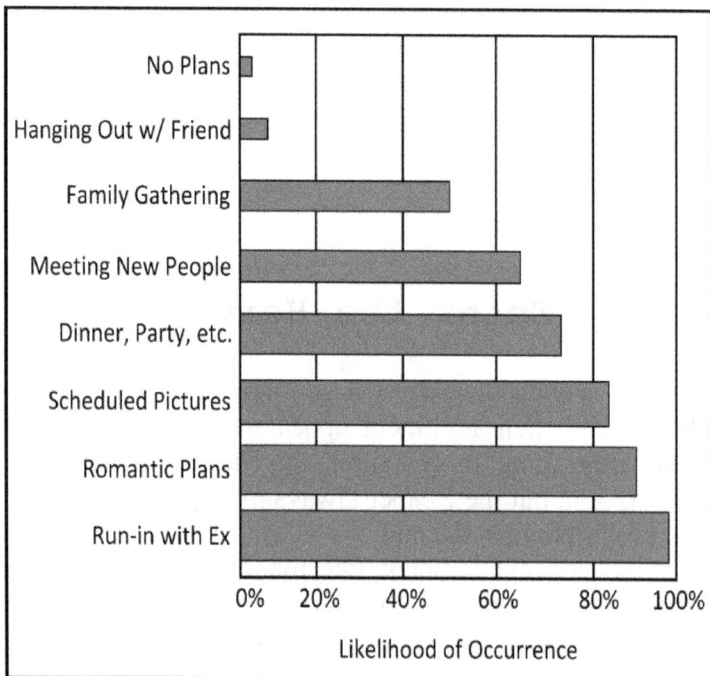

Category	Likelihood of Occurrence
No Plans	~2%
Hanging Out w/ Friend	~5%
Family Gathering	~48%
Meeting New People	~63%
Dinner, Party, etc.	~72%
Scheduled Pictures	~82%
Romantic Plans	~90%
Run-in with Ex	~97%

Likelihood of Occurrence

little overzealous in anticipation of spoiling your social affairs and arrives too early. Mr. Blister might also slip up and get his dates wrong, arriving too late. You should cherish these rare instances, but take care not to mock the herpes, lest you wish being subjected to a more fearsome wrath on a subsequent visit.

While you are tainted, your blister will pass through several stages. I hope you want to know what they are because I have listed them below.

1. Humble Beginnings: the prodrome stage in which you experience the tingle of things to come. Use this warning to make preparations.

2. The Peak of Freshness: Bubbles! Normally the word brings a smile to one's face, but I believe we can all agree this is one exception. Welcome to the springtime of your lip visitor's life cycle. In this stage, your budding blister blossoms into a pustular and ulcerative monstrosity.

3. The Final Bow: called "Scab City" by some, this is Act III of the performance when the blister has reached its crusty conclusion, but hangs around indefinitely, possibly expecting requests for an encore. During this phase you must take care with everyday movements such as smiling or yawning. I also recommend not scheduling a visit to the dentist. Lip scabs are not flexible.

Before going any further, I would like to direct your attention back to those two wonderfully vivid adjectives mentioned in Stage 2: "pustular" and "ulcerative". Think about those words. Why not take a moment to say them out loud?

6

Under the Influence

Fellow "herpites" (that's a cute little nickname for those of us infected) are probably familiar with the topic covered in this chapter, but I will elaborate for those who have a herpite in their life so they may better understand and thus be more empathetic.

Speculation, that is not entirely vast, suggests you are more susceptible to your dark side while your face is adorned with a fresh blistering. This school of thought proposes that since fever blisters come from the "Dark Place", you are more likely to demonstrate behaviors uncharacteristic of your usual demeanor. For instance, you might ignore a friendly coworker attempting to make small talk, you might blatantly cut someone off in traffic or you might not replace the toilet paper roll on purpose (though it only takes about 10 seconds). Furthermore, it is believed an outbreak of multiple blisters compounds your unbecoming potential.

A freelance (unlicensed) behavior specialist, who may or may not be me, believes such actions stem from a temporary mental condition that only occurs in the victim when a fever blister is on display. This condition is called the Herpes Complex. Get it? Herpes simplex, herpes complex. But in this regard the word "complex" refers to…oh forget it. The basic tenet of Herpes Complex is those with a decorated lip believe others view them with heaping amounts of fear and disgust.

One blistery individual confided to me that she believes cashiers don't want to take her money, as if she is suffering from leprosy and has been carrying the bills around in her mouth. Such thoughts lead the fever-blistered person to lash out in revenge, even if aversive actions or negative comments have not been conveyed. If this sounds all too familiar, remember you must resist the temptation. Giving in to the darkness allows the herpes to feed on your negativity. Be nice, people.

7

Treatment

Obviously there is no cure for face herpes or this chapter would have no purpose. While a range of treatment options exist, I have been informed the pills that require a prescription are most effective. Some suspect the various creams on the market are actually wicked accelerants designed to exacerbate the herpes, and more often than not, these substances are nothing more than branded placebos. This unusual conspiracy theory suggests you are provided a false hope of "treating" your herpes while, in fact, you are simply allowing the little guy to reach his full-blown crusty potential.

Members of the famed Fever Blister Community (hereafter referred to as FBC, though that reference may never be used again), have access to a range of secret techniques and creative treatments. If you are not yet a member, rest easy. These unofficial options will be made available to you forthwith.

I suppose we should start simply with a couple of tactics for disguising your little visitors. These methods should be obvious, but I can't assume everyone has the same well of knowledge. Some might be walking blind in the world of herpes.

The employment of makeup is one of the most basic cover-ups. Sexist types might view this approach as a strictly female form of fever blister camouflage, but there is no such thing as gender roles when you're combating a face crustacean. If you're a battle-hardened veteran, you know sometimes you have to change up your tactics. For instance, let's say you have an important presentation for work in your immediate future. You don't want your audience paying more attention to the latest corruption of your mouth, right?

Either gender should be advised the practice of using makeup depends heavily on the location and stage of the herpes. If the blister is in the Peak of Freshness, you're good to go no matter the location. Onlookers with a keen eye might be suspicious, but your stowaway will go mostly unnoticed. If you have progressed to Scab City, you risk raising a big red herpes flag if you try to cover it up. I don't use the makeup trick myself. I like for everyone to behold my herpes unmasked, in all its glory, throughout the dastardly duration. Not really. I prefer to utilize the following method.

Afflicted victims of the male persuasion should feel especially fortunate as they can make use of a wealthy mustache (provided they can grow one) to conceal their crusties behind a curtain of facial hair. Now someone might ask, "But what if it's on my lower lip?" Well, just grow your mustache longer…if you can.

If simply masking the herpes is not feasible or does not mesh with your personality, you can take a more forward-thinking approach. The next couple of ideas are for those of you who prefer tackling the objective of desensitizing others to your outbreaks.

A particularly bold approach is to snatch up a pen or marker and draw a little circle around your latest face cultivation. This alleviates the pressure from people you interact with and bypasses those awkward moments when you catch them spying at your herpes. As I'm sure you're already aware, the eyes of the uninfected are unexplainably drawn to the presence of a fever blister. You know they see it, but they don't want to say anything and they're doing their best to avoid making eye contact with it due to fear of infection. By flagging your crusty appendage, you save them the trouble and you can launch into a discussion of it immediately.

You might also consider flashier moves such as color coordinating your clothing to really make your fever blister "pop". I recommend earth tones such as reds and browns, but I'm sure you can find other color schemes that will compliment your lip growth. Claiming your herpes as a fashion accessory confuses others into accepting it.

I will now discuss a couple of the creative treatment techniques I delightfully teased earlier. The first I have not tried myself, but I've heard this method is effective in "shrinking" the target. Are you ready for this? It's hemorrhoid cream. That's right. And I'm going to assume if you're feeling adventurous or desperate enough to test this particular strategy, you'll need a cover story as to why you're buying that special cream. Or maybe you'd rather not have a cover story. Weirdo.

If your willingness to treat your herpes is of a hardcore nature, you might be tempted to dab rubbing alcohol on your blister with a cotton swab to speed the drying process. I have personally engaged in this activity on countless occasions. It's invigorating.

Community extremists have entertained the notion of liquid nitrogen as a potential form of instant treatment. Those discussions quickly ended when the matter of supply and the high risk of accidents came into question. Acid and fire were likewise considered.

With the preceding information so fresh in mind, I hope you realize you are not as limited when dealing with your bubbly buddies as you might have been led to believe. You don't have to rely on so-called "treatments" at the local drugstore. And gone are the days of hiding behind a surgical mask or quarantining yourself to spare friends and family the horror of your hideous visage.

8

Fun with Fever Blisters

Uninfected individuals don't know what it's like to face the discriminating eyes of those who are "grossed out" by fever blisters. This chapter showcases several methods designed to lessen the humiliation of being tagged by the herpes. These ingenious coping mechanisms range from simple and humorous to those with cash money potential. No one in their right mind considers time spent with a fever blister as enjoyable, but there's no reason you can't make the most of it.

As mentioned earlier, you might find delight in the act of applying funny nicknames to your fever blisters (not necessarily in place of medication, but that's really up to you). You can expound upon this idea by delivering messages from your fever blister to friends, family or coworkers. For example, during a phone call you could say, "My crusty buddy says hello" or "I've got a little friend looking forward to seeing you at Thanksgiving".

If you happen to fancy yourself a crafty person, custom greeting cards or postcards with pictures of you and your herpes are a swell idea for friends and family. You might deliver such messages as "My lip lover and I wish you were here", "My dark visitor and I hope you get well soon" or "My lip critter and I would like to congratulate you".

Another activity you might enjoy is creating a detailed documentation of your outbreaks. If you're so inclined, this hobby would entail photographing your various herpes happenings and then organizing those memories into scrapbooks, photo albums or a handsome coffee table book. You might even go so far as to slap a catchy title on the front. Something like "My Herpes Through the Years".

The next couple of ideas are exclusively for those who have obtained unwanted custody of herpes simplex. One of these "members only" options takes a page from the twelve-step programs. Organized meetings provide an opportunity for people who do not have a network of fever blister friends to connect with others suffering from the same condition.

Each person in attendance would have a turn to introduce themselves ("My name is _____ and I have fever blisters") and then share their story. This group setting serves to educate the herpes handlers that they are not alone and no longer need to feel like they belong in the shadows. And in place of sponsors, participants could hook up with a "blister buddy" to remain in contact with outside of the meetings for additional support.

You could even take the previous idea a step further and involve friends and loved ones. In this scenario, the social network of the fever-blistered would be given the opportunity to talk about how the random yet routine presence of the herpes has affected their relationship, love life, etc.

Saving the best for last, the other exclusive activity for lip scab recipients is the Fever Blister Lottery. Now before you get too excited, you should know this game requires contact with a circle of other fever blister folk to participate. In particular, you'll want to play this game with people you will see regularly on holidays or other special occasions.

Prior to an upcoming event, everyone participating in the lottery makes a wager they will receive a gift from the Fever Blister Fairy just in time for the designated occasion. Whoever is fortunate (and equally unfortunate) enough to show up with a nice bubbly spread takes the pot. In the event of a tie, which might very likely be the case, the money should be distributed evenly amongst the winners. If, by some strange twist of fate, no one shows up with a spoiled mouth, then just add the cash flow to the pot for the next event of your choosing. Based on past experience, I'm guessing you won't have to worry about that.

I pray you have been inspired by one or more of the suggestions covered in this chapter. I'm sure you and your crusty-lipped cronies can develop more activities designed to inject some fun into your instances of fever blistering. And as you may have realized, these are all tactics to bring unexpected attention to the herpes and thus demoralize it in a passive-aggressive way.

Epilogue

Your quest for fever blister wisdom is now complete. I would like to think you are backstroking lazily through a warm, euphoric calmness with the realization you have assorted options in the land of herpes simplex. Or the case may be you are envious after reading this happening handbook and you desire to contract some mouth herpes of your own. Well, don't feel left out. If you are meant to have the herpes, it will come to you.

At any rate, I hope you enjoyed the book. Now you are armed with information to aid you in the never-ending battle against the face darkness. Become a herpes advocate or a fever blister activist. Let your voice be heard and all that jazz. Perhaps one day we will wear our fever blisters with a sense of pride, free from any social stigma attached to the attachments on our lips. Yes, I know that's ridiculous, but perhaps one day others will not look upon our orolabial herpes with such disdain.

Be strong and stay vigilant, friends. The herpes is always lurking.

A Note of Thanks

This fascinating handbook was crafted from all the fever blister jokes and musings my siblings and I have shared over the years. A full-blown, Stage 3 and super crusty 'thank you' goes out to Jimmy Hoskins, Robyn Pagán and Penny Moore for their contributions and support.

And as bizarre as it sounds, I must also give credit to the herpes for inspiring the content. Without HSV-1, none of this would have been necessary.

About the Author

Josef J. Hoskins attempts to give all genres the attention they deserve, but has been accused of showing favoritism toward fantasy and science fiction. He has been an article writer for a couple of websites and his writings have also appeared in a variety of print and online magazines.